THE TECH-SAVVY MANAGER

MANAGER

by

Dan Goldfynn

RELATED WORKS
Easy-to-Read Book Series

Find all at: https://thetechsavvymanager.com

The Tech Savvy Manager

Structured Excel Models

Workbook for Amazon Behaviorial Interviews

1. INTRODUCTION

∞

Have you ever found yourself saying:

"Computers, networks, whatever."

"Those IT guys."

"I don't deal with technology, I'm all about strategy."

"I don't know what they're talking about!"

Perhaps not you, but many people on the business side of things remain completely disconnected from technology. Tech was once "that thing" managed by geeks and existed solely to support business. However, success in business now requires a robust technology strategy, as technological advancements are fundamentally changing how companies operate and scale. This shift presents an inevitable problem — executives and other managers with little knowledge of the technology landscape now have to make complex decisions involving technology.

For instance, do you want to scale your business rapidly online? Suddenly, you have to make a multi-million-dollar decision on *Cloud Transformation* and migrating from your infrastructure, and you have no idea what any of that means.

Feel like you're falling behind in customer experience and clients are defecting to competitors? You're looking at a complex *digital transformation* that will throw a whole bunch of terminology at you and force significant changes to how you run and organize your business.

Are parts of your business complaining about a lack of good analytics and spouting off about *"ML"* and

"Big Data"? Now you have to make decisions about *"AI"* and related topics.

Are your key business process software licenses getting too expensive, and the vendor won't support them anymore? Welcome to the world of *SaaS and PaaS*.

Is your executive complaining incessantly about how slow the IT department is in rolling out new features to consumers? Say hello to *Agile* and *DevOps*.

Confused about this incomprehensible "digital trust"? It's time to talk *Blockchain*.

Most tech-savvy managers realize that these evolutions and revolutions in technology impact not just the IT departments, but they fundamentally change how enterprises operate. These transformations—which are significant shifts, not nudges—require businesses to revisit their strategy, internal and external processes, departmental structures, hiring practices, training, incentives, budgeting, and anything else that has remained unchanged for years. *In such an environment, ignorance about key emerging technologies is no longer a badge of honor—it is a shackle. You run the risk of making decisions or jumping to conclusions about things based on what you think they are rather than what they are.* You also run the risk of falling behind as companies reorganize themselves to leverage technology and value people who understand such concepts.

The purpose of this book is to introduce you to some of the most impactful emerging and modern technology concepts and explain them in very simple terms. Even a basic understanding of these topics can improve your ability to contribute, ask the right questions, participate in related conversations, and increase your stature and positioning in the company.

Each topic is deliberately limited to only a few pages and described in plain language with as few acronyms and technical terms as possible — technology, unfortunately, is rife with acronyms and complex terminology. This approach allows you to absorb and understand the core concepts and then delve more in-depth into any topic you choose. **I am fully aware that** *simplicity comes with a trade-off* **of not adhering to academic definitions, ignoring variants, nuances, and sometimes oversimplifying the complexities behind these concepts and technologies.**

Each chapter covers four broad areas:

A Simplified Definition — explaining in basic terms what the chapter subject means.

The Basics — a more detailed treatment.

Business Application — typical scenarios you will encounter.

Current State — a brief description of major players, industry evolution, resources.

At the end of each chapter, I hope that you will have a basic understanding of what the topic is and how it might apply to your business. It's perfectly acceptable not to understand every term or remember every detail. You should feel no pressure to "know it all."

I hope you find this book useful in your journey to becoming technically aware and advancing your personal and professional goals.

2. TERMS PRIMER

∞

If you're a novice when it comes to technology, don't worry. We all have areas where we're beginners. I commend and thank you for choosing to learn here. Please take a few minutes to familiarize yourself with some terms that we will use frequently throughout the rest of the book.

Applications

Applications is a generic term for all software that users utilize to perform tasks. Microsoft Word, the games you play, the code editor used by your company's developers, your browser, Adobe Photoshop—all of these are applications. Applications run on an Operating System (OS).

Operating Systems

An Operating System (OS) is software that runs on hardware and allows you to build and/or run applications on it. You might be very familiar with an OS without necessarily knowing what it is. Windows 10, Mac OS Mojave, Ubuntu Linux, iOS, Android— these are all OSs, and they allow you to run all your applications.

Compute

Compute refers to devices with the processing power and memory to run OSs and applications. Your laptop, desktop, servers (specially designed computers that reside in data centers and basement units), mobile devices, and even your Apple Watch, are all part of the "compute" infrastructure.

Storage

Storage is where your data resides—your hard drives, USB sticks, large databases—all the infrastructure that holds information. Your "Compute" typically comes with storage or connects to storage. Storage can be persistent (like hard drives) or temporary (RAM—chips in your computer that lose all information when powered off). You can have fast storage (SSDs—solid state devices) or slow (your spinning hard disk). There are many other concepts, classifications, and types (like Network Attached Storage, and Storage Area Network), but this should suffice for the basics.

Network

Network encompasses all the pipes, plumbing, and protocols that connect various devices. That router in your home, the strange antenna boxes in the company closet, sophisticated gateways, switches, and load balancers (don't worry about what they are), the fiber network and circuitry that connects your offices to other offices and the Internet—all of this falls under the classification of "Networks."

Security

Security includes all the software, devices, and appliances that help keep your networks safe from intrusion and damage. An appliance is a term used for a device that runs specific software and plugs into your network.

Physical

Physical refers to all the other "stuff" that's needed for IT infrastructure to run—like the buildings, utilities, security teams guarding the facility, and support teams.

Let's look at a few other important definitions.

Data Centers (DC)

Data Centers are large, custom-designed buildings that house vast arrays of servers, storage, and networking equipment to connect to the internet highways. You could call your air-conditioned basement a Data Center, and in a way, it is. However, when we say DC, we're referring to larger facilities.

Data Centers have custom cooling, redundant power connectivity to the equipment, dual power feeds to the facility (sometimes), specialized security and monitoring, and protection from natural events (floods, earthquakes). They also serve multiple purposes; some host numerous companies (e.g., an Amazon AWS data center serving thousands of companies) while others are custom-built and serve a single company (your company's dedicated data center).

Data Centers are usually categorized as Tier 1, 2, 3, 4 by the Uptime Institute based on several parameters typically related to redundancy. Type 4's are the most sophisticated.

Most technically adept companies tend to replicate their data between multiple DCs. That way, even if one DC goes down, there is an immediate failover to a distant, secondary DC, and the company can continue to operate with minimal downtime.

Workloads

A workload is anything that requires a certain amount of processing power for an application to run at a given time, serving a certain number of users. When someone says, "we need to migrate that workload," what they're saying is "some other place needs to have the equivalent processing power to run the same thing." This term is used quite heavily in Cloud-related discussions.

Now that you're armed with the basics, it's time to dive in.

3. CLOUD

∞

This chapter is fundamental to understanding a lot of what we will discuss in this book. Cloud computing, at scale and available for anyone to use, was pioneered by Amazon. Amazon was using complex server configurations to support their massive retail operations when someone proposed, "Why not also rent this infrastructure for others to use?" Now, AWS (Amazon Web Services) is Amazon's fastest-growing and most profitable division. It has paved the way for numerous followers and transformed the IT world. Amazon introduced the term "cloud" along with its "Elastic Compute Cloud" product in 2006.

Cloud computing is fundamental to most emerging technologies and acts as the backbone for almost every new concept you hear about. Having a basic knowledge of what the Cloud is (and isn't) will help you better appreciate most other chapters, especially when I refer to Cloud computing, scale, efficiency, and so on.

Simplified Definition

The "Cloud" is on-demand, highly scalable, compute, storage, and network infrastructure, bound by specialized software, that you can pay per use. Think of it as a complex IT infrastructure available as a service.

The Basics

"The Cloud" is everywhere. You can't escape phrases like "run it on the Cloud," "migrate to the Cloud," and "Public Cloud." Amazon talks about the Cloud,

Google is shouting about it, Microsoft is chirping about it, Salesforce runs on it, and tech pundits keep pontificating that "The Cloud" is transforming IT. But what is it?

"The Cloud" is large-scale computing infrastructure available on-demand. This infrastructure runs in a data center, either owned by a specialist company (e.g., Amazon AWS) or your own.

However, what makes the "Cloud" unique compared to a cluster of computers in your company's basement? The answer lies in how that cluster is used and made available for people who need it. It's easier to explain by covering three distinguishing characteristics of the Cloud:

1. Available On-Demand
2. Scalable
3. Continuously Evolving

Available on Demand

This means you can buy, configure, and use resources on demand. Don't need a certain amount of processing power and storage this month? Don't pay for it. Need more resources in the morning than in the evening? You can get it when you want. Is your seasonal demand very high in December? You can get extra computational capacity just for the month to handle your spikes without having to buy, manage, and refresh all that hardware.

Let's get a little technical: The most common resources needed are processing power (CPU and RAM), storage, and data transfer bandwidth (M/Gbps). You will often hear the term "instance," for example, "I need an instance of a machine with 4-cores,

6 GB RAM each, with 125 GB high-speed storage per instance." You use this instance to run your virtual machines and applications (we will cover virtualization later in this book). And when you don't need the resources, you can "turn them off" and not pay for the off-minutes.

Scalable

Let's say your business is growing fast, and you need to add 100 new servers to handle all the traffic and software needs. In the past, you would take five months to release an RFP, go through a painful selection process, and deal with all the headaches associated with buying, installing, managing, maintaining, and retiring those servers. But with Cloud infrastructure, you can add those resources in literally minutes using a web browser, and they are available for you to use. That's because the Cloud provider has plenty of resources ready and available on-demand, and makes these resources available through simple, browser-enabled configuration. You can choose the instance sizes (they're often called T-shirt sizing, like M, L, XL) with a few clicks, and minutes later new computing power is available for your developers and operations engineers to use.

Constantly Evolving

The benefit of centralized Cloud is that the Cloud company can continuously evolve and improve features from which you can benefit. Strong security, geographical replication, load balancing, and tons of other features (including all the major new technologies mentioned in this book) are at your disposal and available as and when you need them.

There are different Cloud configurations you will hear about, and they're not Cumulus, Nimbus, or Cirrus.

Types of Clouds

There are four prominent Cloud configurations, and most complex transformations involve more than one. Let's demystify them.

Public Cloud

This refers to any Cloud that's provided by an external provider and available for anyone. Resources are carved out for you from a large shared pool that's also used by many other companies. Your data is safe and fenced off from the others, but the overall infrastructure is shared.

Because Public Clouds are huge (e.g., AWS, Google, Microsoft), you get lower prices due to their economies of scale, and they also tend to be at the forefront of technological improvements. Even certain other vendors, like Oracle and SAP, are building their own clouds and encouraging customers to move their desktop products to their cloud versions.

Private Cloud

Private Clouds are set up separately for you. A third-party company will buy infrastructure and host it in a data center (or a colocation center), and then charge you for usage, or they provide a closed network "carve" of their capacity dedicated only to you. No one else except your company has access to the infrastructure—and any excess capacity is not shared with any other company. The third party will take care of all design, maintenance, upgrades, and retirement, and you get similar features as a Public Cloud. You will typically pay higher prices for private clouds because the providers have to custom-build and maintain it for you, and they do not enjoy the same economies of scale as the large Public Clouds.

Companies use Private Clouds for a variety of reasons — like when they want to run highly customized or sensitive software, have very high-performance requirements, need to manage security-intensive data, or want ownership of hosting facilities.

Hybrid Cloud

A hybrid Cloud is a mix of the above two. A conduit connects the private and Public Cloud and moves data between the two. Why do people use a hybrid? Well, sometimes it's cheaper to use Public Cloud for things that the company doesn't insist must be within its complete control, so that part moves to the Public Cloud and the rest stays private. Companies sensitive about their data but also budget-conscious typically use this approach.

For example, IBM may build a private Cloud for you and connect it with Amazon AWS. IBM would manage everything, but you would get some price benefits because a portion of your workloads and data might reside on Amazon's infrastructure.

Most large enterprises tend to have a mix of public and private clouds due to the complexity of their landscape, the diverse mix of legacy and modern systems, regulatory compliance requirements, and sometimes just the lack of budget, time, and resources to move everything off of their private infrastructure.

Community Cloud

This is more like a Private Cloud, except that this is usually shared among similar organizations—for example, the Government Cloud.

Cloud Conversations

Here are four common Cloud-related discussions that you will encounter.

1. *Cloud Migration*—Moving workloads from your existing legacy data centers to the Cloud— this can be complex and time-consuming, so you should be thoughtful about the questions you pose and understand the extent of the migration. An important aspect of migration is how your organization's current state differs from the future state. When you move significantly to the cloud, your current IT organization has to look different and needs to be manned by people with different skill sets, and the mindset of how you operate as an IT function changes. One should be aware of the impact it has on organizational setups and processes after the migration.

2. *App Modernization*—This is about retiring or changing your old/outdated enterprise and desktop applications, but modernization conversations almost always involve a significant amount of Cloud Migration and moving towards SaaS (which you will read about later in this book). Without going into details, it is helpful to know that not everything can be moved to the Cloud, and there is almost always a Cloud readiness assessment. There are

various reasons why something cannot move to the Cloud, like the application architecture, legacy designs, hardware limitations, etc., but if someone says "we can move everything to the Cloud," then it's worth challenging that assumption.

3. ***Cloud Optimization*** — This is all about examining the costs and performance on the Cloud, and then figuring out the right contracts to ensure you are not paying for what you do not need. Cloud optimization can be tricky.

4. ***Public Cloud vs. Private/On-Premise*** — There will, many a time, be discussions on whether your applications are better off on your On-Premise systems or the Cloud. This is especially critical when your applications are very specific, need low latency, extremely high throughput, or have any other proprietary characteristic that cannot be met by a Public Cloud provider. In these discussions, the conversation is not just about cost, but also whether your applications can run on the Cloud. By focusing on costs, you might miss critical bottlenecks related to your application architecture.

When it comes to contracting, Cloud contracts can be pretty complicated, and they usually come in two flavors — fixed (1-year, 3-year) or truly elastic (pay-per-use), and charges are often by "virtual instances," which is the general term for a compute unit that comprises a certain amount of processing power, memory, and storage. There are several in-betweens, so don't be surprised if you are ever asked to look at a Cloud contract.

One of the common pitfalls in the excitement around Cloud is that executives automatically assume that moving to the Cloud means saving money. That is not always the case! It is possible that the move is even net-neutral; however, the move will enable a whole new set of possibilities and scale to your business which otherwise would be impossible. Also, poorly designed migrations and poor oversight of Cloud run costs can lead to leakage and wasted money, so you have to be wary of any promise of guaranteed saved money.

Business Benefits

We've covered several benefits as part of the conversation already, but here's a short list of some of the key business benefits of Cloud:

1. Reduced operational costs and simplified operations when deployed correctly
2. Ability to scale operations rapidly with a growing business
3. Access to a wide variety of emerging tools and technologies built on the cloud
4. Reduced *(not eliminated)* security risk and associated fallout costs
5. The ability to transition from CAPEX to OPEX

Current State

Cloud at this point is ubiquitous — it is pretty much a commodity. Almost every major enterprise today runs workloads on Public or Private Clouds. The most profitable and fastest-growing businesses in Google

("GCP—Google Cloud Platform"), Amazon ("AWS—Amazon Web Services"), and Microsoft ("Microsoft Azure") are their Cloud divisions. It is no longer a question of "do we need Cloud," but "where do we need it, how much, and how do we want to pay for it."

While most of this chapter talked about Cloud in infrastructure terms, later on, we will be covering many things that run on the Cloud as they are part of the Cloud computing ecosystem.

Cloud computing has transformed the entire IT landscape, and if you think your company is far behind or has not embraced it, it is time to have those conversations. Almost all the emerging technologies covered in this book are predicated on utilizing Cloud infrastructure because those new technologies require scale, agility, massive amounts of storage, computing power—all that the Cloud stands for.

Now that you hopefully have somewhat of an understanding of the Cloud, let's go and learn about all the things that are built on top of this Cloud.

4. XAAS — IAAS, PAAS, SAAS

∞

XaaS, or "Anything-as-a-Service," is a model where you pay for a service on a subscription basis. Subscriptions are typically (though not always) based on the number of users, the number of minutes used, or the number of license seats purchased, and are charged on a monthly basis. Most of these services offer the option to purchase capacity upfront for a committed timeline (like a year) in exchange for attractive discounts.

Consider the three aaS' in a layered structure — this is a simplified explanation to give you an idea of how these concepts are positioned against each other.

At the bottom is IaaS — which represents infrastructure.

In the middle is PaaS — which represents platforms running on that infrastructure, on which you can build, run, manage, and monitor applications and services.

And on the top is SaaS — which represents end-user applications available as a service.

However, keep in mind that as a business, you can subscribe to each layer independently of the others, depending on your specific purposes and needs.

IaaS — Infrastructure as a Service

IaaS essentially involves renting cloud computing infrastructure, along with monitoring and maintenance services. With IaaS, which is what most public clouds provide, you rent compute, storage, and network infrastructure. You then place your software and data on this infrastructure and pay a service fee for its use. The advantage is that you don't have to worry about buying, managing, maintaining, or retiring the hardware, although you are responsible for everything that runs on that hardware. IaaS is also great for companies that prefer to avoid capital expenditures and instead want to move to an operational expenditure model.

PaaS

PaaS, or "Platform-as-a-Service," is perhaps the most complex of the three aaS'. PaaS services provide a platform on which developers can build, run, monitor, and manage applications without the complexity and headache associated with building and maintaining the underlying infrastructure required to build and run those applications.

Let's revisit the concept of the "application stack."

1. First, you need applications that users use (like your company website, or your software product).

2. Then, you need the tools, programming languages, databases, web servers, and all other associated "software stuff" to build and run those applications or widgets.

3. And finally, you need infrastructure (remember IaaS) to host those tools and "stuff" on which these applications run.

PaaS represents the middle portion—it reduces the headache associated with building and running applications.

What's the headache, you might ask?

Well, to build sophisticated applications, run and maintain them, you need an execution environment, web servers, monitoring services, cache, databases, test automatons, queues, profilers, loggers, plugins, APIs, and a host of other things. Not only that, you have to manage and maintain all these various components, their versions, patches, upgrades, security holes—all of which can be great time wasters, resource suckers, and frankly a horrendous pain in every place. Typically, developers and operations engineers tend to create (or cobble together) all this infrastructure and tooling to build and run their apps, and they suffer all the pain that comes with it.

So, the question for every software department is, do they want their expensive software developers to spend 80% of their time dealing with platform issues, or do they want them to spend their time coding their applications?

That's where PaaS comes in. Products like Heroku, Amazon AWS, Microsoft Azure, and Force.com all provide a comprehensive suite of "platforms" on which developers can build and run their applications while availing supporting features, without worrying about anything underneath. They can focus on writing code, testing, deploying, and monitoring the app instead of spending all their time managing, maintaining, and cobbling together a platform on which to build and run the app.

In essence, you have cloud computing infrastructure, ON WHICH you have platform features, ON WHICH developers build and run applications, WHICH your users use to do their thing.

SaaS

SaaS, or "Software-as-a-Service," is a model where you pay subscription fees for applications that are managed by a third-party vendor.

Let's delve a little deeper. Consider how you dealt with HR, Payroll, Supply Chain and Logistics, etc., in the past. These were either home-grown applications, spreadsheets, or expensive, customized ERPs (Enterprise Resource Planning software like SAP). Over time, they became unwieldy, requiring armies of developers or contractors to keep them up and running and to add new features. You had to buy new hardware to run them and keep up with growth, and they became a real drag on businesses getting distracted by system issues.

Enter "SaaS," which are essentially full-featured applications running on the cloud. Take Workday, for example. Workday provides most HR and recruitment features, and companies typically pay per seat (i.e., the number of users on it). The great thing about this is that the company behind Workday ensures that the software is continuously managed, has new features, backs up data, provides training, creates mobile apps, and all other work to make sure the product is robust, continuously updated, and available on any number of devices and operating systems. All you do is pay per month for use, and everything else is taken care of. This is great for many companies because they can now focus on their business rather than trying to become a software house. The important thing to note here is that all your data is now with Workday on their data centers, managed in their cloud, and you access your company-specific portal, usually on a web browser.

You may have heard of many SaaS products without ever thinking of them as SaaS. Here are some popular examples:

- Salesforce

- Wordpress.com

- Microsoft Office 365

- Adobe's Creative Suite

- Concur Travel

- Shopify

- Ariba supply chain

The benefit of SaaS is that companies, no matter what their size, can take advantage of top-quality, full-featured products, without breaking the bank or creating large, unwieldy IT departments. A 20-member startup can avail the same rich suite of sales applications on Salesforce as a 100,000-employee behemoth.

Target Audiences

Another way to understand XaaS is from a target audience perspective:

1. SaaS—regular users, support departments, basically anyone that wants to use an "app."

2. PaaS —developers, architects, testers

3. IaaS—Operations engineers, system architects, data center managers, IT administrators, network engineers

Remember, it is not necessary that SaaS or PaaS products run on the same IaaS you purchased. You may have purchased some cloud IaaS to do "stuff A," and you may have purchased subscriptions to Salesforce, a SaaS which would be running on Salesforce's Data Centers and has nothing to do with your IaaS. These are concepts, and within your company's context, the products you purchase in each layer are not required to be dependent.

Business Applications

Almost every major company and startup today uses one or more XaaS products and services. The guiding principle for any company considering a XaaS route is whether they should be in the business of IT and managing applications. If the answer is no, then perhaps using a XaaS feature is in order.

Business Benefits

1. Simplified development and deployment

2. Reduced operational costs & maintenance challenges

3. Access to the latest and greatest tools and technologies to enhance development and user productivity

4. Improved user experience and satisfaction

Challenges

There are some challenges to be aware of when going the XaaS route.

1. Getting specialized talent to configure and customize for company-specific use can be difficult. Configuring your IT departments to have a few specialists, while leveraging external consulting companies, is one way enterprises manage this challenge.

2. Departments can lose track of how much they are paying for subscription fees and realize too late that they are paying for what they are not using. Therefore, you should periodically audit your subscription expenses and have departments justify usage. You should consciously turn off seats and resources that you do not use.

3. The challenge of choices — every few years there's the next shiny thing that feels so much better, easier, cheaper than the one you have, but moving away can be a significant challenge due to the stickiness.

XaaS may not always reduce your overall cost (you will pay in subscriptions and customization what you previously paid for your employees), but it will bring efficiency to your business operations and let you focus on the core competency of your business, which has significant upsides to your revenue generation and margins.

5. VIRTUALIZATION & CONTAINERIZATION

∞

Druva's virtualization survey noted that 90% of respondents said they would be running Virtual Machines (VMs) in the Cloud...

Now we're delving into more technical territory. But then again, you're aiming to become a tech-savvy manager!

First, let's tackle virtualization. This concept, whether you've heard of it or not, is pervasive in the Cloud world. In fact, virtualization is what makes the Cloud possible at scale. Without it, data centers would have to be miles long, cost ten times more, and the services would be so expensive that it would all make no sense.

Before we dive deeper, it's important to note that while virtualization makes economical Cloud possible, there can be virtualization without any "Cloud stuff." For example, an individual's desktop running three Virtual Machines has utilized virtualization, and this configuration has nothing to do with "The Cloud."

Intrigued? Let's continue.

Virtualization, in the context of technology, is the creation of a virtual resource (such as a server) that can be replicated on an underlying physical resource. The most common virtualized resource, which makes Cloud scale possible, is a virtual Operating System (Virtual OS).

To understand this concept, let's consider what the world without virtualization looks like. The simplest example? Your work or home laptop.

Your laptop is a physical resource. On this physical resource, you may be running an OS, like Microsoft Windows 10, Mac OS X, or one of the flavors of Linux (like Ubuntu). It's one unit, and all your applications run on the OS.

But let's say, for some reason, you want to run a few applications that are only available on another OS. You have Mac OS, and you want to run Windows, but you don't want to buy a new laptop or uninstall your Mac OS. What do you do?

That's where virtualization comes in. A piece of software called a "Hypervisor" abstracts the interface between a host machine (your desktop) and the OS, allowing you to install an entirely different OS on it.

Here's how it would work:

1. You install a Hypervisor on, say, your Apple MacBook.

2. Then you install Windows 10 on the Hypervisor.

3. When you need to access Windows 10, you launch the hypervisor and then launch the "Windows 10 Virtual Machine," which essentially creates a window like any other app, but is actually Windows 10. You can use Windows 10 like a regular machine and run your apps on it.

In this configuration, you have two OS's running on your laptop, one of which is a VM.

Now, if your computer is powerful enough, you might be able to run three additional OS's apart from your primary Mac. *What you've done is "virtualized" your environment.*

Let's extend this concept to a test engineer. Instead of buying three computers for her to test an app on different OS's, she can now run three different OS's on the same machine through virtualization software. It's a whole lot cheaper and efficient.

Now let's extend this to the Cloud world. Most Cloud configurations will have a certain number of physical servers in the Data Center, but each physical server runs multiple VMs (Virtual Machines) on them — this is what we call "VM density," which allows one to take full advantage of all the resource capacity on a machine. This means that a Data Center with 500 servers can, in effect, behave like it is running 1,500 servers (due to a VM density of 3 in this case).

One point to note: When you run an OS as a VM, it's still a full license. Your OS license costs don't go down; however, you don't need to buy another machine to run the OS.

Power Up and Power Down

In the Cloud section, I talked quite a bit about how you can use Cloud resources "On Demand." Well, here's how it really happens (simplified, of course).

The Cloud company purchases, say, 100 servers.

On them, the company installs 1,000 VMs (x10 density), each with a certain resource allocation (like processing power, RAM), so that the 1,000 VMs are sharing the power of the one hundred units of underlying physical hardware.

You can turn off the VMs when you don't use them, and not pay for those minutes when the VM is not running on the hardware. When you power off the

VMs, the act frees resource capacity on the underlying server, and the Cloud company can now let someone else use that capacity (not the specific VM instance, that one's yours). This explanation grossly simplifies what is happening and how, but that is the gist of it.

So, the Cloud company is really maximizing the usage of its hardware, and instead of one hundred applications running on one hundred servers, they have managed to run a thousand, and you get to share some of the benefits of that saving.

Containerization

You may have heard about Containerization. You're probably thinking, wait, what now? Wasn't Cloud, PaaS, IaaS, SaaS, VM enough?

Well, this topic is best described within the space of Virtualization, though they aren't quite the same.

A "Container" is a self-sufficient "bundle" of an application and everything needed to run it, which you can then take and run anywhere on a supporting OS. Many argue that Container architecture is more efficient than VM.

What does this mean?

Let's tackle this with a simple explanation.

On your company server, let's say you're running a complicated Linux application—perhaps payroll, or some company-specific inventory web app. Like most apps, this one needs a whole host of supporting components to run—like a web server, plugins, queues, loggers, script extensions, packages—it's a nightmarish landscape of dependencies and dependencies with dependencies! If any one of them breaks, your software stops working.

Suddenly, your server is beginning to fail, it's old, frail, and running on a really ancient version of the OS. IT decides to shift the app to a new server, with a newer OS. And the moment they transfer this app, all hell breaks loose. Half the plugins don't work, and it's all a mess. So, they decide to give up and stay on their old server. Three days later, someone patches a security hole and installs a couple of new OS upgrades, and oops, your app stopped working. Some dependency broke. Back to panic mode again—and this happens far more than you think.

Containerization solves this by letting you bundle the app and all its dependencies into a "container" and then you just transport this "container" to another machine, and it just runs. You don't have to worry about what changed outside the container. The other benefit is that Containers are lightweight, so you can run lots of them on an OS, and they are much faster than VMs to bring up and down. This is because a container runs like an app directly on the OS, whereas a VM runs on the OS and runs the app inside it— creating another intermediary layer between the OS and the app, and adding "heaviness."

Essentially, these Containers let you bundle, ship, and run any application in a lightweight, portable container (duh).

The image below gives you a comparison between a Virtual Machine system vs. a Container system.

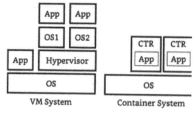

CTR = Container

Let's veer into a slightly more technical comparison; don't worry if it doesn't mean much to you, you can skip it.

VMs represent hardware-level virtualization, whereas Containers are at the Operating System level.

VMs are fully isolated from the surrounding environment, but Containers are slightly less secure as they are essentially running in the same space as other apps on the same OS.

VMs are considered "heavyweight" as compared to containers, which are much faster to bring up and down.

So, in summary, Containers are a great way to bundle complex apps with all their dependencies and run them without stressing over something breaking the app. Docker was the company that pioneered this concept, and they're called "Docker containers."

Business Applications

Most conversations about Cloud and Virtualization also now include Containerization, though it is rare for business managers to get involved in this level of discussion. It's nice to know what Containerization and Virtualization are, and what benefits they bring, but apart from perhaps licensing deals and cost-saving estimates, you should not have to wrack your brains on this topic. However, note that Containers are becoming very popular, and many companies are beginning to move away from VMs and migrating into Containers, so there may be migration discussions.

On the personal end, you can make good use of Containers as well. You can get ready-made Docker packages that you can run (e.g., Plex media server) without dealing with any installation and dependency headaches.

Business Benefits

1. Reduced asset costs and significantly improved utilization.
2. Reduced deployment errors and outage impact.
3. Improved business continuity and Disaster Recovery (DR).
4. Improved development, testing, and deployment efficiency, thereby reducing software development and delivery costs.

Current State

VMs have existed for a long time now, and Containerization has picked up significant steam in recent years. There are a host of companies providing features and products in the space.

VMWare is perhaps the most popular company related to virtual technology. Docker is a pioneer and a very popular Container company/product, and Kubernetes is another well-known Container product.

6. BIG DATA

∞

A NewVantage Venture Partners survey found that 84% of enterprises had launched advanced analytics and Big Data initiatives to bring greater accuracy and accelerate decision-making.

Big Data is a term that gets thrown around a lot. Some people tend to think of it as "lots of data." While it's true that Big Data involves large volumes of data, the volume is just one of the components that characterize what Big Data is.

Before we define Big Data, let's discuss the world before "Big Data" became a significant trend.

Most of the corporate world typically uses RDB — or Relational Databases. The most popular ones are SQL Server (Microsoft), Oracle (Oracle), and MySQL (open source). These databases hold tables that store data in clearly defined columns and rows, with defined types (integers, text, float, etc.). For example, you could have an Employee table with name, ID, age, date-of-hire, and phone number. You could also have another table listing IDs, compensation, organization ID, and so on. You can link these tables and get a single row about an employee in a neat, text-and-numbers format. Traditionally, companies have stored all kinds of important data in these databases — customer data, sales, supply chain, employee, real estate, accounting — anything that's key to business operations.

However, data in the real world is really messy. It is produced in prodigious amounts through people's actions and machine sensors and stored in a variety of places—text files, spreadsheets, PowerPoints, .CSV files, video, image, and audio files, Adobe Photoshop files, database tables, XML files, HTML files, video streams, machine sensor inputs... the list goes on.

Traditional databases do a very poor job of consolidating all these variants. This is because traditional databases require structure (i.e., clearly defined rows and columns for the data they store), but all these different data elements have no rigidly defined structure. It would take impractical amounts of time and resources to scrub these data sources into any type of neat structured table. One webpage is very different from another, one PowerPoint is completely different from another, and so on. There is no clean way to glean insights about what is contained in them because every one of those millions—no, billions—of "data pieces" is different.

You may ask, "What's the pitfall?" Well, structured data is a very small piece of what informs a good view of the subject. Take customers, for example: your database may hold fifty items about a customer in a nice table (name, address, phone number, loyalty card number, preferred store, etc.), but you're likely missing a massive amount of information about that customer. This could include their online presence, their social influence, their job profile changes, their interaction with your partners, the composition of their household, their past interactions with your company, their pattern of behavior to your emails and mails to them, their sentiment when they call your call center—some of it gets creepy, but you get the idea. This information might help you better cater to their needs and proactively address them. But to do that, you need to capture and process massive volumes of both structured AND unstructured data. In the legacy, pre-Cloud computing world, this would be almost impossible due to cost, capacity, and technology constraints.

Enter "Big Data."

Big Data describes a large volume of structured (like the tables we talked about) and unstructured data (all those different format files and streams). This data is usually produced at high velocity and can be mined for information and insights using Machine Learning and other analytical tools.

So, it's about how you get, store, and synthesize these massive volumes of structured and unstructured data the world produces, often at a rapid rate, and get meaningful insights.

Let's take an interesting example of sentiment analysis—how can you determine if your target audience likes your new product? You can, of course, conduct a survey, but it only covers a small population and it's a snapshot in time. But to monitor how people regard your new product release, you can observe all the social media activity, combine that with your retail store footstep performance, combine that with whatever literature people are putting out there on the web, in forms of videos, presentations, dissertations, blog posts, Twitter comments, Facebook and Instagram posts, and whatever else. Then, you analyze all that data to figure out if people are regarding your product positively or negatively. How do you capture all that, in all those completely different formats, synthesize, see patterns, and then generate a trend of your new release's popularity?

Well, you do that by bringing in Big Data technologies to store and sort/synthesize data, and run Machine Learning models to find patterns and trends.

To sum it up, Big Data is not a specific product or a database, but a concept that's made real through a host of tools and technologies. It's a concept of gathering, storing, and analyzing vast volumes of disparate data that is often produced at high velocity.

What Technologies Support Big Data?

Given the scale, velocity, volume, and complexity of storing and processing Big Data, Cloud computing forms the fundamental infrastructural backbone to make it all happen.

Below is a short list of Big Data-related products:

- Apache Hadoop and Spark Processing Engine—makes it easier to store and process massive volumes of data in distributed systems
- Amazon AWS S3 allows you to store massive volumes of data
- Google Cloud DataProc provides a more cost-effective way to run Apache Spark and Hadoop
- MongoDB, Hive, Redshift, and HBase are examples of data systems that let you store or manage structured and unstructured data
- On top of the storage systems, you can run a host of processing, classification, and learning algorithms to make sense of the data

Why is Big Data Important?

Consumers are getting increasingly used to better quality insights and information, and the way to produce better insights is to get hold of disparate, large volumes of pertinent information and process them. Consequently, companies cannot process such data or produce those insights without Big Data technologies.

Let's look at some useful, practical cases of Big Data, not in any specific order of importance:

- Summary View of Customer
- Security & Fraud Prevention
- Sentiment and Loyalty Analysis
- Traffic Management
- Illness Patterns
- Preventive Maintenance
- Network Diagnostics

If your company does analytics, then the natural progression is to improve the richness of analytics through the deployment of Big Data technologies.

An important caveat, one that many engineering teams miss, is that the adoption of these technologies must be use case/business driven rather than technology driven. Don't invest in "Big Data" because it sounds cool; invest because you know what you're trying to get out of it.

Business Benefits

1. Improved business decision-making (for growth or costs) backed by better data and insights
2. Enhanced customer experience and revenue/profitability upside
3. Speed of available information and timeliness of responses

Challenges

1. Lack of clarity on the business case and benefits of deployment
2. Difficulty in recruiting and retaining knowledgeable talent (data science and technology)
3. Growing maturity and rapid changes in the technology and vendor landscape

7. LLMS (LARGE LANGUAGE MODELS AKA CHATGPT STUFF)

∞

Around ~Nov 2022, ChatGPT took the world by storm. For months, you could not scroll through a page on LinkedIn on people either expressing astonishment, admiration, disdain, or excitement around this new technology called "Large Language Models," of which ChatGPT was one implementation, based on a model known as GPT.

Let's delve into this new world.

A Simplified Definition

A large language model is like a digital assistant trained on vast amounts of text. It understands and generates human-like text based on the information it's been trained on. Imagine a super-smart computer program that can answer questions, draft emails, or even write essays by drawing upon knowledge from billions of lines of text–that's LLM for you.

The Basics

At its core, a large language model is an advanced form of machine learning. Machine learning allows computers to learn from data without being explicitly programmed. When we refer to a "language model," we are talking about a program designed to grasp, produce, and interpret human language.

These models are termed "large" because of the enormous volume of data they're trained on. Think of a library with millions of books. Reading all of them would endow you with a vast amount of knowledge. Similarly, these models digest extensive quantities of text, learning patterns, grammar, facts, reasoning abilities, and even a hint of creativity.

The journey of large language models began with simpler models. In the early days, they were trained to predict the next word in a sentence. For example, given "The cat is on the ___," they might predict "mat" or "roof." As research advanced and computing power increased, the capability of these models expanded drastically.

Neural networks, which are computational structures inspired by the human brain, play a vital role in the development of these models. Within neural networks, there's a variant known as "transformers," which have been instrumental in the success of modern large language models. Transformers can understand the context of words in a sentence, allowing models to generate more coherent and contextually relevant sentences.

The watershed moment in this journey was the introduction of GPT (Generative Pre-trained Transformer) by OpenAI. While earlier models could handle short predictions, GPT expanded the horizon by generating entire paragraphs of coherent text. From generating fictional stories to answering complex questions, GPT's capabilities seemed boundless. While most people know about ChatGPT, built on GPT, it's not the only LLM model. At the time of this writing, Google had its own known as "PaLM," and Meta (Facebook's parent) has release LLama. There are many more models, like Claude from Anthropic and Bedrock from Amazon. It is now possible, using Cloud technologies, to even run these models online and train them–for example, a company may choose to run its own flavor of a LLM on the Cloud and train it with its own documentation so that they can build a customer service chatbot that is far more effective in answering customer questions. In a way, the computing scale of the Cloud is *fundamental* to the success of LLMs.

To interact with a large language model, a user usually types a query or a prompt. The model then crafts a response, offering relevant and coherent information or continuation based on its training.

The evolution has been monumental. From models that predicted the next word, we now have digital maestros capable of simulating human-like text generation, answering a diverse range of queries, assisting in creative processes, and much more.

Business Applications

Here are a few examples, by no means exhaustive. You should be able to craft potential applications no matter that your business is. If there was a human contributing to creating content, then LLMs can probably contribute in *some way*, not as a replacement, but as a companion.

1. **Content Creation & Editing**: A media company could harness a language model to draft or refine content. They simply input a topic, and the model churns out a well-structured draft within moments and then humans can refine it.

2. **Customer Support**: E-commerce businesses, inundated with customer queries daily, can leverage language models for instant, 24/7 responses. A question like, "Where is my order?" is met with an immediate status update

from the integrated system. We could extend it to Banks and other consumer-facing businesses.

3. **Market Analysis**: Financial institutions, aiming to gauge market sentiments, can utilize these models. By processing news articles, social media posts, and financial documents, the model can distill a summarized market perspective, facilitating informed decision-making.

Current State

The domain of large language models is evolving rapidly. OpenAI, with their GPT series, is a forerunner, but others like Google's PalM aren't far behind.

The pace at which the industry is advancing is breathtaking. We've leapfrogged from basic next-word prediction models to those executing intricate tasks with ease. The amount of data these models consume to be effective is also staggering and can we can expect increased sophistication over time.

For enthusiasts and professionals alike, resources are plentiful. Academic journals, platforms like Arxiv, tech blogs, and dedicated training platforms provide a wealth of information, bridging the tech-commerce divide.

While the capabilities and applications of large language models (LLMs) are impressive, it's crucial to acknowledge the challenges and disadvantages associated with them.

1. **Bias and Misinformation**: One of the primary concerns is the unintentional propagation of bias. Since LLMs are trained on vast amounts of

data from the internet, they can sometimes reflect and amplify societal prejudices present in that data. For instance, if a model has been exposed to both accurate information and misinformation, there's a risk it might present the misinformation as fact in certain contexts. Not only that, one of the critical issues with LLMs today is "hallucination," that is, the model *simply makes up information*. Relying on LLM answers for factual research can be incredibly risky depending on the sensitivity of the ask. Remember again that this is a *prediction model*, it does not actually know what it is producing is true or false–only that the completion is the *most probable* one satisfying the ask. For example, if you asked "which book did Einstein write?" it is possible that an LLM simply makes up a book, the topic, and the year, all of it entirely false. Be extremely careful in due-diligence if your application of an LLM requires factual accuracy.

2. **Over-reliance**: Businesses may become overly dependent on these models, potentially sidelining human expertise. While LLMs are efficient, they lack the nuanced understanding, emotional intelligence, and ethical considerations inherent in humans. Blind trust in automated outputs can lead to unforeseen errors or ethical dilemmas.

3. **Environmental Concerns**: Training LLMs requires immense computational power, which, in turn, demands significant energy. The carbon footprint of training one of these models can be

substantial, raising environmental and sustainability concerns.

4. **Economic Disruption**: As LLMs find applications in various sectors, there's a potential for job displacement. For example, if a company automates content generation using a model, it might reduce the need for human writers or editors.

5. **Interpretability**: Understanding why an LLM provides a specific answer can be challenging. These models often function as "black boxes," meaning their internal workings and decision-making processes are not always transparent. This can be problematic in sectors where traceability and reasoning behind decisions are crucial.

6. **Security Concerns**: Like any other digital tool, LLMs can be misused. Malicious actors might employ these models for generating fake news, impersonating individuals, or other deceptive practices.

While LLMs present groundbreaking opportunities for various industries, it's essential to approach their adoption with a balanced perspective, weighing their incredible potential against the inherent challenges and ethical considerations. In short, don't rush into it without clearly understanding how you wish to use it and the inherent limitations.

This is a fast moving, fast changing space and undoubtedly poised to bring many changes to various industries–but as all such groundbreaking developments, it is hard to guess the extent of disruption. Government regulations, company restrictions, human adoption or resistance, all will play a role in the evolution of this impressive technology.

In a nutshell: LLMs are wonderful and we should expect significant disruption to our technology-driven world, but are not magic, and not a solution to everything.

8. AGILE & DEVOPS

∞

An HBR article by Bain & Co. noted that Bosch implemented Agile methodology to manage corporate initiatives — an approach that clearly went outside the adoption of Agile in software development.

How many times have you heard of Agile these days? Everything is moving to Agile: Agile development, Agile work methods, and perhaps even Agile ways of eating and forming relationships — who knows!

Before we define Agile, let's take a step back into the world before Agile and visit the most prevalent methodology (which, by the way, is still the most prevalent), called "Waterfall" or "traditional development." This is essentially a sequential development process.

In Waterfall, a project was delivered using a rigid, structured, sequential approach. You had a series of defined phases, you wrote detailed specifications to meet the deadlines for those phases, and at the end of it all, you delivered the application to your customer, whether internal or external. The phases were typically concept, business case, requirements gathering, design, development, testing (integration, system, production), and finally delivery. Anyone who has either approved budgets for these projects or has been involved in one knows that it almost never works this way.

It's challenging to write precise requirements for large, complex software upfront. Things change all the time — user needs, end customer desires, company fortunes, regulatory changes, competitor moves — you never know, and that makes large phases a tremendous pain to manage and deliver. Large phases introduce silos, delay releases, make iteration very bureaucratic and time-consuming, and create armies of program managers whose job is nothing but chasing teams and tracking deliverables. It's inefficient, and in the modern complex landscape where your "app" is no longer just for Microsoft Windows, the whole model becomes a delivery nightmare. Waterfall can work when the target is very defined, narrowly scoped, and clearly understood, but these are far and few in between.

Enter Agile.

"Agile" is essentially a particular approach to project management where the focus is on iterative development and rapid deployment of features in short phases. In Agile, multidisciplinary teams (developers, testers, business counterparts) work together, decide on a set of features to be delivered in short delivery cycles, and then deliver them. I'm simplifying, of course, but *iterative development* is the core philosophy. It makes executives extremely nervous, but that's the new reality.

How is Agile Helpful?

We talked about the pain points of Waterfall. Agile aims to tackle that. Instead of heavy, large, complicated phases, Agile breaks it down into shorter iterative delivery cycles. That way, even though you know you are building a large, complex product, you deliver it in small, sensible chunks with everyone working together. This makes execution more manageable, iterations quicker, delivery faster, and your teams can react to requirement changes quicker by reprioritizing as needed. You are essentially going to market much faster than in a Waterfall.

Agile, when done right, also fosters a spirit of collaboration and urgency. Teams work together — from developers and testers to business teams — all with a clear list of features to deliver in a short amount of time. There is a sense of drive, delivery, and seeing the results of the work, and getting feedback quickly to improve. In these days, when consumers expect great experiences and rapid updates, telling them "wait seven months for the next update" is not going to fly.

So, visually, let's compare a large project delivered through Waterfall (Traditional) vs. Agile.

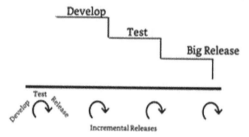

The striking thing about Agile is that it lets you get to the market faster, and then lets you build on your releases, rather than wait forever for one big bang release.

Scrum

You will hear much about "Scrum" — Scrum is essentially a simplified process framework that implements the Agile philosophy. For example, Scrum refers to short development cycles as sprints. If your team follows the Scrum process, they are implementing Agile. There are other Agile frameworks, like DSDM, Crystal, and Kanban, but Scrum is perhaps the most popular.

To summarize—Scrum is one of the popular means by which you implement Agile.

Scrum Definitions

Let's cover a few popular process terms, some you may have heard in the hallway. Note that there are many more, and you will have to read the Scrum Alliance (https://www.scrumalliance.org/) documentation to cover all the concepts.

Sprint

A sprint is a short development cycle—or an iteration of work—during which a select set of product functionality is implemented. An iteration may last about 30 days, during which the teams are fully focused on what is planned for the sprint.

Product Backlog

This is a list of requirements to be prioritized for a sprint. As new features get pushed into a sprint, others stay in the "backlog" until they are ready for development.

Product Owner

The definition of a Product Owner (PO) can get nebulous, but they are essentially the "final authority" representing customer interest. POs are not project managers, but rather the person who will prioritize backlogs for development and ensure they can answer requirements questions from the developers and designers.

Scrum Team

A Scrum Team is a cross-functional group of developers, UX experts, testers, architects — anyone required to deliver the product functionality. These are typically small teams (<10) and it's recommended that they work together in a room. They collaborate and focus on delivering the sprint, with minimal project management and bureaucratic overheads.

Scrum teams are supported by a "Scrum Master," who acts as a facilitator between the team and PO, and typically start a day with a Scrum meeting, and start a sprint with a Sprint planning meeting. Yes, these terms can all get a little tiring.

Release

Not every sprint results in a release. However, when a set of sprints takes the product features to a releasable stage, they may be released out from development to the release pipeline.

Business Benefits

1. *Speed to market* — reach customers early through iterative improvements on your products
2. *Greater customer satisfaction* — through a tighter connection between User Experience and development
3. *Better tech talent retention* — it is more productive and "sexier" to be doing Agile work, and easier to hold on to talent if you're using Agile methodology
4. *Operational efficiency* — reducing development bureaucracy and project management overheads

Now that we've covered Agile as a philosophy and Scrum as a specific framework within that philosophy, let's talk about some common disadvantages and criticisms of Agile.

Disadvantages of Agile

Agile is becoming very popular now, and not everyone knows how to effectively run Agile projects. I have personally witnessed teams calling themselves "Agile" and running their process much like a Waterfall. Just calling your process Scrum and having a "Scrum master" or daily meetings doesn't make the process Agile!

Let's look at some of the challenges:

1. *It's hard to get good Agile talent* — it's a popular philosophy but few know how to do it well

2. *Company mindsets can be archaic* — what do you do when your VP demands an end-to-end project plan with a giant Gantt chart and phase-wise budget? Many companies do not understand the Agile mindset and the concept of iterative development, and the answer of "no, you can't get all features in ten weeks," does not work for many executives

3. *May lead to poor quality software* — this is a complaint, and it can happen if the teams pay lip service to Agile. Furiously pumping out features in short cycles without paying attention to quality and review gates is a recipe for buggy software

4. *Lack of Predictability* — in Waterfall, you went through a pretty rigorous upfront estimation of overall effort and budget. Agile focuses on

chunks and iterations, which can sometimes make it very hard to estimate what the overall effort and budget is, and this can be very frustrating when you hit time and cost overruns

5. *Need for lots of collaboration* — this is the flip side of silos. Many teams have to work closely together, and if your working structure isn't built to collaborate and co-locate, then the effectiveness breaks down and can lead to confusion, frustration, turf wars, and posturing

6. *Leads to poor documentation and project tracking* — unfortunately, Agile creates a mindset of "do quickly, iterate rapidly" which becomes an excuse for "document nothing, track nothing." And the result? When teams move on, the next one has a really hard time maintaining, and projects go off track all under the guise of "Oh, what we didn't deliver this time is coming in the next iteration." Before you know it, the money is over, your contractors have left, and your management is screaming red in the face.

Current State

Agile is very popular these days. Most large companies are beginning to transition their in-house development teams to Agile processes. Most large external consulting and development outsourcing companies are training their armies of developers to work in Agile — including how to make Agile work in offshore/nearshore configurations.

Agile as a concept is also resonating with business leaders, but truly embracing the Agile mindset is still a ways to go in most places. Many struggle with becoming comfortable with iterative developments and the fluidity of long-term planning. In the current complex app landscape arena and rapidly changing customer expectations, Agile is better positioned to help deliver rather than monolithic/rigid traditional processes.

If you have the opportunity, I would always encourage attending an Agile training session if your company offers one, or perhaps even ask some Agile experts in your company to spend two hours talking about it. Most people will be very happy to oblige and share their knowledge.

Now that we've covered Agile in a nutshell, let's talk about another concept called DevOps that works well in an Agile framework (though they are not necessarily intertwined or dependent on each other).

9. DEVOPS

You may have heard a lot about "DevOps." Most people don't really know what it means, and some think it's related to "Agile."

DevOps — an abbreviation for *Development/Operations* — is a methodology that combines Development with Operations.

To elaborate, Development is the phase that involves designing, coding, testing, and releasing to production. Operations takes over from there — building for production, staging, releasing, monitoring, and maintaining the application typically falls under this category. There are nuances, as always, and one can argue where development stops and operations start.

To understand DevOps better, let's examine a world without DevOps, which is the case in most places.

Non-DevOps — i.e., Traditional Development & Operations.

In this scenario, developers ("Development") write code, conduct some testing, and then pass the software to a test team, which performs more detailed testing. Finally, the product is pushed to production, and a separate engineering team ("Operations") monitors the code, profiles the performance, and ensures the application is running smoothly.

Each team is mostly siloed, and release cycles are slow because coordination among these teams is required. Moreover, the development teams have little understanding of the complexities of operations, and vice versa for the operations teams regarding what developers go through.

So, Developers are separate from Operations.

Combine them, and you have DevOps.

DevOps

As the Cloud matured and developers gained access to a rich ecosystem of platforms and tools, it became much easier for developers to use tools traditionally considered "operations" tools. This meant developers could easily push code to production in rapid iterations, stage it for release, monitor and manage the run, all using end-to-end integrated systems that connected development to traditional operations.

The benefit of this is, of course, rapid iterative delivery, more efficient operating structures, and less overhead because most of the DevOps infrastructure is Cloud-supported. One way to think of it is that the Cloud provider has provided an "invisible army" of operations tools and engineers that you can utilize.

DevOps is also becoming very popular, and its challenges are similar to those mentioned in Agile. The biggest adoption challenge is skillset — the availability of engineers and developers who understand how to make it work. The reason DevOps gets combined with Agile is because DevOps is all about rapid, iterative development and release, which aligns perfectly with the Agile philosophy.

An extension of DevOps is DevSecOps — Yes, this stands for Development, Security, and Operations, whereby security checks are integrated into the development pipeline to ensure the delivered product is as secure as possible. So, next time someone says, "We should go do DevOps!" you could respond, "Why not DevSecOps?"

10. BLOCKCHAIN

∞

A survey by Deloitte indicated that while 74% of respondents believed Blockchain could offer a compelling business case, only 34% reported that their companies had initiated any type of deployment. Additionally, 44% of respondents claimed that Blockchain was overhyped, compared to 34%.

Here's another intriguing fact: "The computer power needed to create each Bitcoin consumes at least as much electricity as the average American household burns through in two years."

Among the various topics in this book, the chapter on Blockchain and cryptocurrency might seem the most challenging if I were to delve into the technology behind it. However, fear not. My aim in this chapter is not to delve into the intricate details of the algorithmic concept behind Blockchain. Instead, I will explain what it is and what the future holds in the simplest terms possible. You can always dive deeper into the complex world of Blockchain and cryptocurrency on your own.

In its simplest form, Blockchain is a decentralized distributed ledger, which allows digital information to be distributed anywhere, but not copied. In other words, it ensures that each packet of information (or piece of data) has one owner and that each transaction can be verified. Blockchain is the algorithm that makes cryptocurrency (like Bitcoin) possible, but its applications extend beyond currency.

When companies start discussing Blockchain, the primary goal is to use technology that ensures the trustworthiness of information. How can you function in a highly digital world and transact sensitive information while maintaining absolute integrity over the ownership of that data and all transactions around it without relying on a central certifying authority? That's the kind of issue that Blockchain can help tackle. Cryptocurrency, through Bitcoin, was the first application of Blockchain, but let's examine a few more use cases of Blockchain.

Each case is based on one fundamental principle — the ability to trace transactions and protect primary ownership without the need for a central, certifying authority.

1. Digital record audit trails — particularly useful for banks and other sensitive institutions to maintain robust audit trails of all access to information.
2. Digital ID — secure personal tokens indicating personal ownership.
3. Contracting — exchange of business contract documents.
4. Patient record exchange — sharing of patient records among various hospital systems.
5. Property ownership records — sharing among owners, government agencies, banks, and other interested parties.
6. Purchase records — trail of purchase records in supply chain.
7. Payroll — contract and payment exchange between companies and contractors.

The underlying technology, based on block records and public and private keys, is quite complex and not suitable for this book. To unlock any Blockchain record to conduct a transaction, the owner needs a public key (which is published for anyone to see) and a private key (which only the owner holds). Losing the private key means losing access to the information forever. As a general manager, you are unlikely to need to understand how Blockchain actually works, but it is crucial to have an idea of what Blockchain can do.

Many companies are experimenting with Blockchain, building prototypes and proofs-of-concept to harness the power of this concept. However, we are still a long way from mass adoption. Some of the reasons include:

1. Technical complexity — Blockchain can be hard to comprehend, and all the negative news and hype surrounding Bitcoin and cryptocurrencies create significant hurdles for innovators to paint a compelling picture to executives to secure funding and initiate programs.

2. Lack of compelling, practical use cases — transitioning from hypothetical to real takes several steps, and sometimes the investment does not yield the promised payback. A good analogy is the energy industry — while we all agree that solar power is wonderful, if gas for your house is cheaper, how many would switch to solar?

3. Technology hurdles — Blockchain is too slow for many types of transactions, and many Blockchain networks are not interoperable with each other. This makes high volume, high frequency transaction concepts difficult to implement, thereby hindering large companies from seeing a viable future for their activities.

4. Governance — regulatory clarity and hurdles remain in widespread adoption. The misuse of

cryptocurrency and its association with criminal elements have made regulators wary of the promise of Blockchain, which in turn makes risk-averse industries cautious about what they want to do with it.

Debates continue on cryptocurrencies. The hype of using them as currency has died down somewhat, but companies continue to explore the underlying concepts and where they may apply them.

11. IOT ("INTERNET OF THINGS")

∞

While IoT may sound like a cutting-edge, emerging technology, the term was actually coined in 1999 by Kevin Ashton during his tenure at Procter & Gamble. It was initially used to draw management's attention to RFID (Radio Frequency Identification), a short-range, low-power wireless technology that could be used for tagging items. The term gained mainstream attention nearly a decade after its inception.

Like many other evolving technologies, there is no single, universally adopted definition of IoT. IoT is best explained as the *ecosystem of devices that generate data about their state and location, collect this data via the internet, process the data on a large scale, and drive analytics and action.*

So, what are these "devices"? They are sensors, actuators, cameras, wearables (such as smartwatches and Fitbits), home automation systems, energy meters, asset monitors, and essentially any object equipped with sensors that can generate and transmit data about their state, actions, and ideally, location. Then there are backend systems that collect and process the data for analytics and actions. These backend systems include technologies we've already discussed, like Big Data, Cloud Computing, and Machine Learning (ML). All these elements come together to make the "Internet of Things" possible.

Let's consider an example.

Imagine a complex warehouse and retail delivery system. Every box in that warehouse has a transmitter that relays its ID and location as soon as the box is moved. Now, picture millions of such boxes being moved every day, sending hundreds of millions of data points to a central server until they arrive at a destination warehouse. This central server processes this massive volume of data to provide real-time status to the business and to determine optimal delivery paths and routes. Furthermore, sophisticated visualization can be achieved using Augmented Reality techniques.

Another example is preventative maintenance, where thousands of machines send their performance data for diagnostics, problem identification, and resolution.

Asset tracking, a significant challenge for many large companies, is another area that can be addressed through IoT. Once assets are tagged with sensors, they can be tracked, monitored, diagnosed (where possible), and acted upon until the asset is retired.

This ecosystem of sensors, machines, connectivity, and subsequent analysis is the essence of IoT. What sets it apart from earlier technologies is the sheer scale of data production, particularly through the deployment of sensors, and the consumption and analysis of this data, all enabled through internet-based connectivity. It's worth connecting all the topics we've discussed so far to see how they make IoT possible.

Cloud provides the scale for operations.

Big Data offers the ability to store varied data sources generated at high velocity and prepare them for processing.

Machine Learning (ML) allows for the creation of sophisticated models to sift through and deliver continuously improving insights and action recommendations.

Business Benefits

When implemented with the right business case, IoT can have a significant impact:

1. Improved customer satisfaction
2. Enhanced operational efficiency
3. Better asset utilization and deployment
4. Reduced risk

Current State

IoT is evolving in tandem with the maturity of enabling technologies and the availability of compelling use cases. Manufacturing, Retail, and Health are three sectors leading the way in business adoption.

However, there are challenges in several areas. Here are a few at a high level:

1. Security is a significant concern with all this data being transmitted.
2. The scale of data and processing disparate sources is still too costly for many companies where the business case for doing so is not yet compelling.
3. The cost of devices, procurement, installation, configuration, and management of a large number of sensors can be prohibitive.
4. The ability to hire, train, and retain technical personnel capable of implementing and maintaining modern technologies can be

daunting and expensive, especially for traditional, less technologically advanced businesses (not everyone is Tesla).

12. ROBOTICS & RPA

∞

"Recent research reports show that RPA — Robotic Process Automation — is expected to grow annually at nearly 25% between now and 2023. Another study predicts that by 2025, RPA will perform tasks equivalent to about 150 million employees."

When we hear about automation and robotics, we often imagine robots running amok, computers automating everything, making all jobs redundant, and there's sometimes hysteria about what will happen in the near future.

However, while there's a lot happening in this space, it's not all futuristic science fiction. It's worth understanding the real-world applications.

We'll cover two topics, both with the word "Robot."

Robotics

Robotics is the branch of engineering that deals with the design, development, and construction of robots. Robots don't always refer to moving, automated human or life-like machines, but can also mean computer systems that can perceive via sensors and process the data to control other systems.

The application of robotics is in various stages depending on the industry. It is more prevalent in the military, warehousing, industrial, and healthcare sectors. Robotic arms, bionics, and entertainment machines are some examples in this space. There are also some emerging everyday applications — even your little domestic automatic vacuum cleaner is a simple robot. However, this book is not the right place to discuss robotics as a field — what we are more interested in are the more straightfoward applications of automation in the everyday enterprise, and that is what we will cover in greater detail.

Let's spend a little more time on a more tangible, enterprise-relevant topic that you might come across a whole lot more than dealing with actual robots.

RPA (Robotic Process Automation)

RPA is often confused and misunderstood because of the words *Automation* and *Robotics*.

RPA essentially automates common, high-frequency manually conducted enterprise processes by using software automation agents. But what does Robotics have to do with it? Well, it's because the way the software agents do this automation is by mimicking human actions (clicks, scrolls, app changes, form inputs, enters, auto-fills), but with far greater accuracy and speed. So, it's not about Terminator-style robots filling forms, but usually about software agents that automate some or all parts of a process previously done by humans.

Let's take a real-life example — invoice entering. In many companies, someone from logistics would receive an invoice PDF by email, open it, then open another company app, enter the values from the invoice, and finally hit submit to record it in internal systems.

Enter RPA — a software agent like Blueprism can be used to create a flow of actions, and then let it run. Blueprism (or similar RPA software) then mimics the logistician's actions and completes the process. While the logistician might take 3 hours a day, processing, say, 100 invoices with 4 errors, Blueprism will do it with greater accuracy, say 1 error, and in 5 minutes.

Similarly, RPA is deployed in many enterprise processes that involve one or more manual steps. Here are a few more use cases:

- Statement reconciliation
- Website scraping to pull specific data points and to enter into the company database
- Patient registration and form filling
- Payroll processing
- Transferring data from one system to another by mapping correct fields and correcting spelling errors
- Processing incoming customer query emails and entering information into internal issue tracking systems
- Checking a status website and sending shipping confirmation emails to customers

You get the idea. Any internal process not automated through direct software integration between systems is ripe for RPA automation. But like everything else, not every manual process can be automated! Let's look at when RPA makes the most sense.

1. The process is clear, documented, repeatable
2. The steps are digitized to the extent that they can be automated
3. The steps can be codified in rules
4. There is minimal interpretation of information or human decision-making

5. There are a large number of discrete, simple manual steps, or the process is simple but done a large number of times a day

6. The value of automating is quantifiable/meaningful

If the above characteristics are not met, then the use case may not be appropriate for RPA.

Companies identify RPA use cases by studying discrete manual processes and assessing if the process can be automated. By using the above checklist, you can think of processes in your own department that might be ripe for RPA. Once again, it isn't about fancy robots doing crazy things, but really about how you can save a bunch of clicks and copies in some part of your company processes. HR, Accounting, Finance, and Inventory Management are some areas where RPA is more widely used.

If you have heard of BPO/A (Business Process Optimization/Automation), then most major BPO houses are already automating a lot of the processes handed to them by their clients. RPA improves accuracy, saves time, and reduces costs.

Three companies are leaders in this space, so looking up their websites can be a good primer for learning more about this space and how the tools help realize RPA.

1. Blue Prism
2. UIPath
3. Automation Anywhere

Business Benefits

1. Reduced cost of operations by reducing low-value work and freeing time for more complex work
2. Increased accuracy

13. OTHER CONCEPTS

There are several other concepts that are gaining popularity and traction. While I will not be covering them in this book, you can conduct additional research on them if any of these sound interesting or relevant.

AR/VR — This concept revolves around Augmented Reality and Virtual Reality. For instance, iOS games where you can visualize T-Rex's in your garage, IKEA demonstrating how its furniture would look in your living room, or a hyper-realistic simulation of a roller-coaster are all AR/VR applications. These require the Cloud for large-scale deployments.

NoOps — This concept involves creating a deployment system with "no operations." It takes DevOps to the next level by almost entirely eliminating operations management from in-house developers and engineers.

Microservices — This is an architectural style that structures an application as a collection of independent services connected through APIs (Application Programming Interfaces — a method for two separate systems to communicate using a common 'language'). For example, you might have a service that provides the location of a server based on an IP address, and another that gives a zip code based on an address string. You then build an app that's essentially an amalgamation of all these "micro" services to produce a restaurant app that recommends local places to eat. If you have done any development, think of microservices as you extracting functions from your code, running them separately on a scalable platform, and accessing the response via an API. The benefit of Microservices is that each component can evolve individually, be tested separately, and this makes the overall maintenance and enhancement of the application easier.

SDN — Software Defined Networks — This is a concept where complex networks are defined and managed through software.

14. ONE-LINE SUMMARY

Understanding modern technology can be complex, so let's distill each concept to its essence and explore its potential benefits.

1. *Cloud* — Scalable, on-demand infrastructure.

2. *XaaS* — Software, platforms, and infrastructure as a service, built on the Cloud, for which you pay based on usage.

3. *Virtual Machines* — A virtual computing or storage unit that can be hosted on an existing operating system.

4. *Big Data* — The storage, digestion, and analysis of vast volumes of data produced at high velocity in both structured and unstructured formats.

5. *LLM* — a model trained of vast amounts of text to understand and general human-like language.

6. *Agile* — An iterative, collaborative form of software development that enables teams to release features in short cycles.

7. *DevOps/DevSecOps* — A combination of development and operations in which developers also perform the roles of operations.

8. *IoT* — An ecosystem of sensors that produce high volumes of data, connected to large-scale data processing systems via the internet.

9. *Blockchain* — A decentralized, distributed ledger that provides secure digital ownership and a transaction trail.

10. *RPA* — The automation of manually conducted enterprise processes using software agents.

15. CONCLUSION

The world is changing, and fast. Technology is evolving at a rapid pace and one can no longer distance themselves from this. I hope this book gave you a basic grounding on some key concepts, and now it's up to you to go and dive deep into areas of interest.

Thank you once again for reading, and I wish you the very best!

ACKNOWLEDGEMENTS

Icons made by https://smashicons.com from https://www.flaticon.com

16. RESOURCES

After much thought, I decided it wouldn't help if I linked specific resources as these things change and go stale fast. Instead, I would encourage you to go to the websites of some of the following companies/search terms and dig around and you will find tons of useful material.

Amazon AWS

Microsoft Azure

Google GCP

McKinsey

BCG

Deloitte Consulting

Accenture

CONTINUE YOUR LEARNING JOURNEY
Easy-to-Read Book Series

Find all at: https://thetechsavvymanager.com

The Tech Savvy Manager

Structured Excel Models

Workbook for Amazon Behaviorial Interviews